PRAYING THE LABYRINTH

praying the

LABYRINTH

a journal for spiritual exploration

Jill Kimberly Hartwell Geoffrion

THE PILGRIM PRESS

CLEVELAND, OHIO

The Pilgrim Press, Cleveland, Ohio 44115
© 1999 by Jill Kimberly Hartwell Geoffrion

Drawing of labyrinth by Robert Ferré. Used by permission.

Biblical quotations are from the New Revised Standard Version of the Bible,
© 1989 by the Division of Christian Education of the National Council of
Churches of Christ in the U.S.A., and are used by permission. Adaptations have
been made for inclusivity.

Printed in the United States of America on acid-free paper

09   08   07   06   05   10   9   8   7   6

Library of Congress Cataloging-in-Publication Data

Geoffrion, Jill Kimberly Hartwell, 1958– .
    Praying the labyrinth : a journal for spiritual exploration / Jill Kimberly
Hartwell Geoffrion.
        p.   cm.
    Includes bibliographical references.
    ISBN 0-8298-1343-8 (pbk. : alk. paper)
    1. Spiritual life—Christianity.   2. Labyrinths—Religious aspects—
Christianity.   3. Meditations.   4. Labyrinths—Religious aspects—
Christianity meditations.   I. Title.
BV4509.5.G45 1999
246.4'6—dc21   99-34495
                                                                          CIP

Contents

Foreword

IT TAKES COURAGE to go on pilgrimage. Even if your destination is self-chosen and your trip tailor-made to meet your needs, it still takes courage. You, as pilgrim, leave your familiar world behind, bid goodbye to your loved ones, and walk into the unknown.

This book is a result of Jill Geoffrion's courageous journey to Chartres Cathedral in France. Her experience of being with and walking the magnificent eleven-circuit medieval labyrinth is reflected in every page.

What is a labyrinth? It is a path of prayer, a walking meditation that can become a mirror of the soul. The labyrinth at Chartres is a forty-two-foot circle cut into the stone floor. It has one single path that meanders in a circuitous way from the entry to the center and back out again. It was placed in Chartres Cathedral sometime between 1194, after the Great Fire, and 1220, when the Fulbert section of the nave was rebuilt. The path becomes a metaphor for our own spiritual journey. A labyrinth is not a maze. A maze is designed for you to lose your way; a labyrinth is designed for you to find your way.

Many of you may have walked a labyrinth, and will move into these pages with ease. If you are not familiar with the labyrinth, this is a wonderful way to acquaint yourself. Meditate on the selections. Allow the pattern to seep into your pores as a way to prepare to walk a labyrinth sometime in the future.

This unique book is designed for you to experience your experience. It is in a meditative, workbook format that allows time and space for you, the reader and seeker, to nourish your creative urges, to reflect on questions that trouble or excite you, and to find the holy spaces in your life. Jill has organized the book in two sections, Readying and Opening, with many areas under each section. You can start from the beginning or simply go to a topic that grabs your attention. Allow this book to give you a "time-out" from your ordinary day.

Reflect, ponder, enjoy . . .

—Reverend Dr. Lauren Artress

Acknowledgments

With gratitude to God, who invited me to Chartres, France, and faithfully traveled with me.

Tim, my husband and soul mate, who gave me the pilgrimage as a birthday gift and later helped refine my manuscript.

All those who prayed with me as I prepared and journeyed.

Robert Ferré, whose commitment to being a pilgrim set the stage for much learning and praying.

Tim and Dan, my sons, who supported me from afar, even when it felt lonely.

Kate Christianson, for her faithful and faith-filled prayers on my behalf.

Elizabeth Nagel, who shared the journey with me.

Elizabeth Toohey, my spiritual director, whose wisdom and insight helped me to be well prepared.

Lauren Artress, whose leadership made the pilgrimage possible.

Kris Nourse, who sent a handsewn heart along with me to remind me of my commitment to keep my heart open throughout the pilgrimage.

And to my fellow pilgrims: Alan, Angela, Anika, Anne, Betty, Bill, Charlotte, Donna, Elizabeth, Hank, Janet, Jenny, Jimmy, Kristin, Lauren, Marietta, Mary, Mary Lee, Midge, Nancy, Pat, Robert, Ruth, Sandra, Sonia, and Tom.

Introduction

BEAUTIFUL SPIRITUAL TOOL
—a pattern, an emblem, a walkway—has captured my attention and my heart. The labyrinth is its name. If you are seeking to know God more deeply, then this journal will support your creative explorations. Nurturing spiritual growth in many different ways is one of its primary goals. Challenge, support, and surprise are built in.

If you have never walked a labyrinth, this journal can introduce you to this wonderful way of praying. If you are seeking to enhance the praying you do with labyrinths, this journal can be an aid and companion.

JOURNEYS WITH THE LABYRINTH

This book is the fruit of a pilgrimage I made to pray with and on the pavement labyrinth on the floor of Chartres Cathedral in France. When I returned, I sat down at the computer and prayed, "God, please use my experiences to enrich others' lives." Having no clear idea of how I wanted to proceed, I took out my pilgrimage journal and began to read. Poems spontaneously emerged. These in turn invited questions about spiritual

exploration. As I continued to attend to the dialogue between my experiences and queries, echoes of biblical texts filled my mind. I inserted
them at the appropriate spots, realizing for the first time that they had
enriched both my pilgrimage in France and my manuscript. The image of
the labyrinth belonged with the words I was using to reflect on it. It
needed to be in the midst of each selection, just as it had been in the
midst of each encounter I had in Chartres.

I first learned about the labyrinth during an interview with an artist
about her experiences of prayer. Since I was unfamiliar with this way of
praying, she later sent me an article about the labyrinths at Grace
Cathedral in San Francisco.

I was taken aback just by viewing the outline of the labyrinth. I knew
deep within that I was looking at Truth in a symbolic form. Intrigued,
I enlarged the diagram of the labyrinth until I could "walk" it by hand.
Within seconds of placing my finger on the pathway I was aware that the
labyrinth was mirroring the story of my spiritual journey. Suddenly I un-
derstood my unfolding relationship with God more deeply. I felt a surge
of relief and gratitude that remains with me to this day.

Even though the labyrinth is designed to be experienced bodily, I felt
no need or inclination to walk a labyrinth; being with it visually was
enough. However, it was important to me to have copies of the labyrinth
design around—above my desk, in the kitchen by the phone, on earrings
that I wore.

Three years after I first saw a labyrinth, my family traveled to San
Francisco. When I realized we were going to be near Grace Cathedral, I
knew it was time to pray the labyrinth with my feet.

What I experienced in walking my first labyrinth has forever changed
me. On one level, it was a typical family outing. We walked the labyrinth
together but in our own ways—some meditatively, some skipping or run-
ning, some filled with curiosity and questions. On a far deeper level, I was
surprised by the experience. I was pulled in to a spiritual exercise that,
now, I cannot imagine living without.

Six months later I received the gift of a trip to Chartres Cathedral in
France to walk the labyrinth there. In preparation I began walking a local
labyrinth whose outline had been mowed in the grass outside a spiritual-

ity center. The more I walked the labyrinth, the more I loved the process. I couldn't explain why this form of praying was becoming so important to me, yet I knew that it was bringing together many years of study and practice of prayer and devotion.

BEING DEEPLY CONNECTED

Two truths about labyrinth praying guided me throughout my pilgrimage and opened the door to many rich experiences. The first was a deep, intuitional knowing that there was no "right" way to pray the labyrinth. The other was that God is very present in the midst of labyrinth praying.

As I walked the labyrinth I felt deeply connected to a creative God whose energies resonated in my mind, my whole body, my emotions, and my memory. The form of this book reflects my experience. Each entry begins with a poetic account of one of my learnings with the Chartres labyrinth. These were inspired by times of quiet reflection at Chartres Cathedral, presentations by lecturers on the Chartres labyrinth, and actual experiences of walking the labyrinth.

The echoes of beloved sacred texts are coupled with each poem. On the page, as in life, they are held together by the labyrinth. A question that came into being through the interaction of my praying, the labyrinth, and biblical echoes is also offered.

In many beautiful ways the labyrinth has enriched my own life and the lives of those I love. My prayer is that this book will be your invitation to walk the labyrinth so that you can experience more deeply than ever the love and wisdom of God.

PRAYING THE LABYRINTH

PART ONE

readying

All guides cite the cathedral at Chartres as a model of aesthetic achievement. But the master-craftsman was seeking something quite other than this. He was not creating Art but a cathedral. He was trying (and succeeded) to construct an instrument of religious action, direct action, having in itself power over [people]; a power to transform and transmute.

It is a means of passage from one world to another; a bridge between two worlds which, geometrically speaking, express themselves differently. It is a passage from the straight to the curved, as difficult to bring about as the marriage of fire and water. And it would seem that it is this successful transfer from plane to the curve, this magic in the negation of weight by weight, this tension in stone that generated energy; this subtle projection of a celestial harmony that lives in matter, that is responsible, through [people's] grossest and subtlest senses at the same time, for this action.

Unless [one] is totally impervious, whoever has seen, or visited, Chartres is saturated with it, no longer quite the same [person] . . . the old "crucible" has not lost all of its power.

—Louis Charpentier, *The Mysteries of Chartres Cathedral*

GETTING READY

Journaling Supplies to Be Gathered

A book with blank pages
Pens
Colored pencils—24 pack
Double-sided colored markers (broad tip/thin tip)
Scissors
Double-stick tape

My approach
to this journal
is to record
whatever,
whenever,
wherever,
however.

It helps me
to externalize
my feelings
and thoughts.

Jesus said to them, "Therefore every scribe
who has been trained for the reign of heaven is like
the head of a household who brings out of his or her
treasure what is new and what is old."
(Matthew 13:52)

What will you need to express the feelings and thoughts that will emerge as you journey?

Why
am I going
on this pilgrimage?

I have dreamt of walking the Chartres labyrinth
since I first saw its design.
But there is more . . .

I sense profound longing.
"For what?"
I ask myself.
I can't explain.
I don't know yet.

I'm trusting
that if I go,
I'll find out later.

As a deer longs for flowing streams,
so my soul longs for you, O God. My soul thirsts
for God, for the living God. When shall I come and
behold the face of God? (Psalm 42:1–2)

In the Beginning . . . Are the Questions

What are you longing for?

God is inviting me
to travel to Chartres Cathedral
and to walk the labyrinth there.

I can't say why—
yet.

Beyond a doubt
I am certain
that this wasn't my idea
first.

Now God said to Abram, "Go from your country and
your kindred and your father's house to the land that I
will show you. . . . So Abram went." (Genesis 12:1, 4a)

Knowing the Most Important Things

What is bubbling up from deep within? To what is God inviting you?

MY INTENTIONS FOR MY PILGRIMAGE TO CHARTRES

It is my intention to trust the process of preparation
    as it unfolds in my life
and to follow the path that becomes clear before
    me as I go.
(Twelve weeks prior to my pilgrimage)

It is my intention
that my behavior and choices will reflect
my acceptance of God's invitation to use this
    pilgrimage as a personal retreat.
(Eleven weeks prior to my pilgrimage)

It is my intention
to be and to honor who I am whether I am with God,
    myself, or others.
(Ten weeks prior to my pilgrimage)

It is my intention
to remain open to the Divine.
(Nine weeks prior to my pilgrimage)

It is my intention
that when I feel/sense/intuit God's presence,
    I will ask to be taught.
(Eight weeks prior to my pilgrimage)

It is my intention
to respond to God's invitations to grow and
    to become more whole.
(Seven weeks prior to my pilgrimage)

It is my intention to be myself in the
    deepest ways possible.
(Six weeks prior to my pilgrimage)

It is my intention
to spend more time praying than thinking
    while I am on the pilgrimage.
(Two weeks prior to my pilgrimage)

It is my intention
to seek silence, stay aware of my breath, honor interior
    spaces, and write when it feels right.
(One week prior to my pilgrimage)

I intend to keep on reminding you of these things,
though you know them already and are established in
the truth that has come to you. (2 Peter 1:12)

CLARIFYING YOUR INTENTIONS

What intentions support you?

I am ready to leave for Chartres,
but I feel deep sadness
that I go without my family.

Tears well up
as I say goodbye.
I wish we could all go together.

Yet I know
this is a journey
I must make alone.

So I pray:
"Lover of My Family,
I entrust
Tim,
T.C.,
and Dan
into Your care."

Jesus went up the mountain by himself . . .
(Matthew 14:23)

LETTING GO; LETTING GOD

What feelings and needs do you want to leave with God as you move forward?

An open heart
and
receptivity
are the two things
I have committed myself to pray for
while I'm on pilgrimage.

God and I have been in conversation for months
about what I wanted to pray for the most.

An open heart
and receptivity—
these are my deepest spiritual desires.

> You desire truth in the inward being;
> therefore teach me wisdom in my secret heart.
> (Psalm 51:6)

PRAYING YOUR DESIRES

What do you feel most drawn to pray for?

As I was signing up for my pilgrimage to Chartres
I gave the travel brochure about it to a friend.

Within a week I got a call.
"God seems to be pretty persistent about wanting me to go,"
she reported.
Elizabeth signed up shortly after I did.

On the plane flight from Minneapolis
my friend sits
one row in front of me.

"I am happy to be near Elizabeth.
I appreciate togetherness and separateness,"
I note in my journal.

Two months before I left, Angela called.
"I know it's your pilgrimage," she said,
"but I think God may be inviting me too.
How would you feel if we journeyed together?"

I was excited!

I write:
"As I fly to Newark airport I make a space in my heart for Angela."

> Terah took his son Abram and his grandson Lot,
> son of Haran, and his daughter-in-law Sarai, his son
> Abram's wife, and they went out together from Ur of
> the Chaldeans to go into the land of Canaan. . . .
> So Abram went, as God had told him; and Lot
> went with him. (Gen. 11:31a; 12:4a)

WELCOMING OTHER PILGRIMS

How do you want to relate to those who travel with you on your spiritual quest?

I filled out a request form at church yesterday
asking for prayers for my journey.

The "pray-er" of the day
spoke to God of my pilgrimage
as a transition.

Transition to what?

Therein lies the adventure.

God came and stood there, calling as before,
"Samuel! Samuel!" And Samuel said, "Speak, for your
servant is listening." (1 Samuel 3:10)

TRANSITIONING

How would your journey be different if you approached it as an adventure? Buckle your seat belt!

PART TWO

opening

"The Chartres labyrinth was laid into the cathedral floor sometime between the Great Fire of 1194 and 1220. . . .

The labyrinth is located in the west end of the nave, the central body of the cathedral. When you walk in the main door and look toward the high altar, you see the center of the labyrinth on the floor about fifty paces in front of you. It is approximately 42 feet in diameter and the path is 16 inches wide. The total walking path is 861.5 feet in length. Unfortunately, because it is covered with chairs many people who have visited Chartres have not even noticed it.

Despite the chairs, you can still see the center of the labyrinth which lies in the center aisle of the cathedral. It is a circle about nine feet in diameter with six discernible petals. At Chartres, the center looks like a large scar in the floor. The original centerpiece of the labyrinth was made of copper, brass, and lead. It was removed during the Napoleonic Wars and used to make cannonballs.

The singular path of the classical eleven-circuit labyrinth lies in eleven concentric circles with a twelfth being the center of the labyrinth. The path meanders throughout the whole circle. There are thirty-four turns on the path going in to the center. Six of these are semi–right angle turns, and twenty-eight others are 180-degree U-turns. The number 12 is important in the sacred arts. It is the multiple of 3, representing heaven, and 4, representing earth. The path overall represents creation.

The center of the labyrinth is often called the rosette. It is made up of a six-petaled rose-shaped area.

There are ten labyrs in the classical eleven-circuit labyrinth. They are the double-ax symbol visible at the turns, found between the turns throughout the pattern. Labyr is believed to be the root word of the word labyrinth. . . . When you look at the pattern as a whole from above, they form a large cross, a cruciform.

Lunations are the outer ring of partial circles that completes the outside circle of the labyrinth. They are unique to the classical eleven-circuit labyrinth in Chartres Cathedral."

—Lauren Artress, *Walking a Sacred Path: Rediscovering the Labyrinth as a Spiritual Tool*

APPROACHING CHARTRES CATHEDRAL

All this way . . .
Thousands of miles . . .

For what
have I come all this way?

(Deep breath.)

To look.
To see.
To know.
To be known.

God of All the Earth,
Thank You
for coming with me.
Thank You
for being here.
Thank You
that I can be here
with You.

I am like a green olive tree in the house of God.
I trust in the steadfast love of God forever and ever.
I will thank you forever, because of what you have done.
In the presence of the faithful I will proclaim your
name, for it is good. (Psalm 52:8, 9)

Connecting on a Deeper Level

Pay attention to your body. Can you perceive any tension? Take a deep breath and let it out slowly. What do you want to say to God now?

I studied art history on site in Chartres Cathedral
during my college Junior Year Abroad in France.

Many years later I heard
there was a pavement labyrinth on the floor at Chartres.
I couldn't believe it! I had absolutely no recollection of it.
I kept wondering,
Did I learn about the labyrinth and not pay any attention?
Or, did I miss seeing it completely?

Now, bringing my question with me back to the cathedral
    twenty years later,
I realize that I never noticed the labyrinth when I was here before!
One strip of it is partially exposed by space made for an aisle,
but the rest remains hidden by the wooden chairs that sit on top of it.

I never was aware of the labyrinth during my previous visits.
Totally oblivious of its existence, I walked right over it!

Now I have come back with eyes that see beneath the chairs.

> Now on that same day two of them were going to a village
> called Emmaus, about seven miles from Jerusalem, and talking with
> each other about all these things that had happened. While they
> were talking and discussing, Jesus himself came near and went with
> them, but their eyes were kept from recognizing him.
>
> As they came near the village to which they were going, he
> walked ahead as if he were going on. But they urged him strongly,
> saying, "Stay with us, because it is almost evening and the day
> is now nearly over." So he went in to stay with them. When he was at
> the table with them, he took bread, blessed and broke it, and gave it
> to them. Then their eyes were opened, and they recognized him; and
> he vanished from their sight. They said to each other, "Were not our
> hearts burning within us while he was talking to us on the road,
> while he was opening the scriptures to us?" (Luke 24:13–16, 28–32)

APPROACHING THE SACRED AGAIN . . . FOR THE FIRST TIME

What is it time to notice and let in?

The question springs
from the center of my being:

What other holy ground
am I walking over
and not noticing?

What "chairs"
sit on top of holy invitations
that I have yet to perceive?

Open my eyes . . . (Psalm 119:18a)

FINDING A QUESTION TO LIVE WITH

What "chairs" sit on top of God's invitations to you?

Leaving my hotel
I walk up the hill to the cathedral.
I enter from the back
and go find a chair where I can sit quietly
in the labyrinth's presence.

After a while
I go stand
in the center of the labyrinth.
Just stand.

I inhale the air that
touches the labyrinth's face.
I exhale, kissing it with my breath.

Some thoughts come,
but I don't write them down
or reflect on them.
I let them go.

I want to feel the full extent of my gratitude
at having arrived
at this destination
that has lived in my heart for so long.

Being present is such a gift.

The place on which you are standing is holy ground.
(Exodus 3:5b)

GREETING THE HOLY

(Put everything down.) Be present to your experience of this moment.

Our personal explorations of Chartres
are enriched by various presentations.

As I learn more about labyrinths
I jot down these phrases:

"Be open and follow,
the labyrinth will take you places you don't expect."

"Just present yourself without expectation or demand."

"The labyrinth is one answer to the question,
Do you know where I can find God?"

> Ask, and it will be given you; search, and you will find;
> knock, and the door will be opened for you. For everyone
> who asks receives, and everyone who searches finds, and
> for everyone who knocks, the door will be opened.
> (Matthew 7:7–8)

PAYING ATTENTION

Identify the thoughts, feelings, phrases, images, and questions that are shaping your spiritual journey. Jot down as many as you can think of.

I return to the cathedral
whenever there is discretionary time in our group's schedule.

Internal and external energies mingle
as I draw
while sitting on a chair which rests on the labyrinth.

I hear someone behind me trying to get my attention.
A man leans over my shoulder so that I feel his breath on my neck.
He laughs loudly as he sees that I am outlining a foot.

I understand and even appreciate the humorous response,
but I resent his uninvited presence.

I choose not to respond outwardly to this man's invitations to engage,
hoping this intruder will get the message that I want to be alone.
But he lingers, as close as ever.

I turn around slowly and intentionally,
giving him a look that communicates my desire for solitude.

I turn back and, regaining my focus, begin drawing again.

"Cursed be anyone who moves a neighbor's
boundary marker." All the people shall say, "Amen!"
(Deuteronomy 27:17)

HONORING YOURSELF

What personal space do you need? What boundaries can you establish to help you stay focused?

Last night
I dreamt
of an enormous lush green hillside.

It was four-tiered,
sloping downward in four directions
toward a distant plateau.

In the center
was a labyrinth,
exactly the same shape and size
as the Chartres labyrinth.

The whole scene—
as viewed from above—
felt so full of life.
It beckoned me to come.

God came to Laban the Aramean in a dream by night.
(Genesis 31:24)

DREAMING

What gifts are coming to you in the form of dreams? Record the images and feelings that are beckoning you.

I hear one of the facilitators of our pilgrimage saying,
"The labyrinth is your tool."

I have known the labyrinth as
a way of prayer . . .
a beautiful pattern of Truth . . .
something ancient with modern relevance . . .
one of God's dwelling places . . .
a container for religious ritual . . .
but have never recognized it as one of my spiritual tools.

With this insight stoking the fires of my creativity,
I am filled
with longing,
hope,
and most of all
excitement.

O God, all my longing is known to you.
(Psalm 38:9a)

SPIRITUAL TOOLS

What spiritual tools do you use to find hope and joy?

I often approach
labyrinths straight on.

I walk up to the mouth
and enter directly.

Yet I am hearing from
those who walk around
the labyrinth first.

Maybe once.
Maybe twice.
Maybe more times.

They are saying that this
helps to somehow "contain"
the experience.

By circumambulating
they feel more prepared to
receive the gifts given on the
winding path.

I want to try this out.

Moses sent them to spy out the land of Canaan,
and said to them, "Go up there into the Negeb, and go
up into the hill country, and see what the land is like,
and whether the people who live in it are strong or
weak, whether they are few or many . . ."

So they went up and spied out the land.
(Numbers 13:17–18, 21)

Trying It Out

What movements do you want and need to make in order to receive the gifts that are awaiting you? What are you waiting for? Do them!

The lecturer is speaking of the labyrinth
as "an incredibly powerful problem solving device."

I've experienced what he means.
Yet the dynamism I feel in the labyrinth's presence
leads me to other expressions of this truth.

If I wanted to say something about using the labyrinth
to help solve a problem
I would suggest:
"The labyrinth
is a place to be with a problem
in the energetic presence of the Divine."

Likewise the Spirit helps us in our weakness;
for we do not know how to pray as we ought, but that
very Spirit intercedes with sighs too deep for words.
And God, who searches the heart, knows what is the
mind of the Spirit, because the Spirit intercedes for the
saints according to the will of God. (Romans 8:26–27)

BEING PRESENT TO A PROBLEM

Where do you need to go so that you and God can work together? What will you explore there?

When I look at the labyrinth,
it is as if I were gazing through a clear glass window
right into the beautiful face of God.

"Come," my heart says, "seek God's face!"
Your face, God, do I seek. (Psalm 27:8)

LOOKING DEEPLY

What do you see as you look at the labyrinth?

"The soul thinks in images,"
says Joseph Campbell.

Chartres Cathedral is full of images . . .
which ones does my soul feel drawn to?

Candles burning
as symbols of prayers left behind,

White doves, encircled by blue,
flying in the huge north rose window,

The statue of the crowned Mary and Jesus,

Mary's shroud, the cathedral relic,

The 110-foot well in the crypt,

The Black Madonna with an oak-leaf crown,

but most of all,
the pavement labyrinth on the floor.

Jesus said, "With what can we compare the reign of
God, or what parable will we use for it?" (Mark 4:30)

NONVERBAL KNOWING

What images nourish your soul?

"God geometricizes,"
a labyrinth maker tells me with conviction.

If it is true
that God works through
patterns,
shapes,
and numerical relationships,
what should I be paying attention to
as I spend time with the Chartres labyrinth?

> God brought me, in visions, to the land of Israel,
> and set me down upon a very high mountain,
> on which was a structure like a city to the south.
> When God brought me there, a man was there, whose
> appearance shone like bronze, with a linen cord and a
> measuring reed in his hand; and he was standing in
> the gateway. The man said to me, "Mortal, look closely
> and listen attentively, and set your mind upon all that I
> shall show you, for you were brought here in order that
> I might show it to you; declare all that you see
> to the house of Israel." (Ezekiel 40:2–4)

CAN YOU IMAGINE?

What patterns or shapes have sparked your imagination lately?

As our group of pilgrims prepares
to walk the labyrinth tonight
I am informed
that the floor of the cathedral
is filthy.

"If you want to walk without shoes,
keep your socks on.
That way your feet won't get dirty,"
I hear.

I want nothing more than
to make direct contact—
skin to stone—
with the labyrinth.

Dirt or no dirt, I will take off my socks
and place the soles of my feet
reverentially on the cool cathedral flagstones.

Remove the sandals from your feet,
for the place on which you are standing is holy ground.
(Exodus 3:5b)

MIND-BODY-SPIRIT

What types of direct connection is your body seeking?

After dinner our group gathers at the labyrinth.
Each of us enters, proceeds to the center, and retraces our way out.

"I can no longer care what other people think,"
pops into my awareness
as I finish
walking the labyrinth
in Chartres.

I repeat the phrase internally:
"I can no longer care what other people think."
"I can no longer care what other people think."
"I can no longer care what other people think."
"I can no longer care what other people think."
"I can no longer care what other people think."

As I welcome this gift
into both my mind and my heart,
I bow
toward the center of the labyrinth in reverence
to God who delights in using this spiritual tool.

"All the presidents of the kingdom, the prefects
and the satraps, the counselors and the governors are
agreed that the king should establish an ordinance
and enforce an interdict, that whoever prays to anyone, divine or human, for thirty days, except to you,
O king, shall be thrown into a den of lions."

Although Daniel knew that the document had
been signed, he continued to go to his house, which
had windows in its upper room open toward Jerusalem,
and to get down on his knees three times a day to pray
to his God and praise God. (Daniel 6:7, 10)

GETTING THE POINT

Who are you being called to become in spite of others' opposition or lack of understanding?

We walk the labyrinth after hours when the cathedral is empty.
This allows us to walk it more than once a night, if we want to.

On the path out of the labyrinth
my body notices
that some of my woundedness has been healed!

I feel and perceive that I have left
deeply painful parts of my history
with God
in the center.

I did not set out to release my past.
I did not even notice that I was letting go.
I was simply aware of a profound connection with the Divine.

But now . . .
as I reflect,
as I pray,
I find myself different.

I am amazed
and deeply grateful.

> I will give thanks to God with my whole heart;
> I will tell of all your wonderful deeds. I will be glad and
> exult in you; I will sing praise to your name,
> O Most High. (Psalm 9:1–2)

BEING WITH GOD

How have recent connections with God surprised and changed you?

Words elude me
as I emerge from the labyrinth.

I take out my colored pencils.

Blue swirls
represent the center
where I stood gratefully
in the midst of
Divine acceptance
and forgiving love.

In this sea of blue
I gave to God
a piece of my brokenness.

Red lines—
some curved,
some straight,
some long,
some short—
represent the places
along the second half
of my labyrinth journey
where I felt a longing to take back
that which I had left
in The Center.

The thought of my affliction and my homelessness
is wormwood and gall! My soul continually thinks of it
and is bowed down within me. But this I call to mind,
and therefore I have hope: The steadfast love of God
never ceases, God's mercies never come to an end;
they are new every morning; great is your faithfulness.
(Lamentations 3:19–23)

DRAWING THE TRUTH

Bring into your awareness a recent spiritual experience. Express it without using words.

Surrounded by the stories of the Christian Scriptures
told in the colors of stained glass,
I feel present to the God of the Bible.

I am especially drawn to the white birds
in one of the rose windows.

They remind me that after Jesus was baptized
a dove descended on him
and God spoke the words,
"This is my Son, whom I love;
with him I am well pleased."

With this story resonating inside
I walk the labyrinth.

In my heart I hear God's voice echoing,
"You, Jill, are my beloved daughter,
whom I love;
with you I am well pleased."

What a gift!

For we did not follow cleverly devised myths when
we made known to you the power and coming of our
Lord Jesus Christ, but we had been eyewitnesses of his
majesty. For he received honor and glory from God . . .
when that voice was conveyed to him by the Majestic
Glory, saying, "This is my Child, my Beloved, with
whom I am well pleased." We ourselves heard this
voice come from heaven, while we were with him on
the holy mountain. (2 Peter 1:16–18)

THE VOICE OF GOD

If you heard God's voice saying to YOU,
"YOU are my beloved child, whom I love;
with YOU I am well pleased!"
how would you respond?

Early in the morning,
before the others are finished with breakfast
I come to be with you, Labyrinth.

In an attempt to know you more fully
I choose a different part of you to rest on
each time I arrive.

It feels so nurturing just to sit with you;
you are a safe home place.

May I open my heart
even wider
to you, Holy Circle.

Return, O my soul, to your rest, for God
has dealt bountifully with you. (Psalm 116:7)

RESTORATION

What do you feel as you rest in God's presence?

Labyrinth, I return with gratitude.

Last night as I entered your path
I found myself looking down—
working to stay within your lines.

When my neck got tired from bending
I began moving forward
without trying so hard,
trusting your path to lead me.

What a difference!
What a surprise!
I felt more sure of where I was going
and who I was becoming.

Thank you!

Make me to know your ways, O God;
teach me your paths. (Psalm 25:4)

FINDING YOUR WAY

If you were to relax and trust the path you are on, what might you discover?

Our pilgrimage group is learning
several simple chants
from the ecumenical Taizé community.

Tonight as we walk the labyrinth
we will sing the familiar words of Scripture
"Stay with me,
Remain with me,
Watch and pray . . ."

Many embodied voices
chanting one song.
Many journeys
on one path.

Be filled with the Spirit, as you sing psalms
and hymns and spiritual songs among yourselves,
singing and making melody to God in your hearts,
giving thanks to God . . . at all times and for everything
in the name of our Lord Jesus Christ.
(Ephesians 5:18b–20)

MUSICAL OPENINGS

What music or song would enhance your spiritual journey today? Do you need to sing or hum it? Listen to it? Play it? Compose it? Do so now, paying attention to what the music evokes in you or calls you to.

Circumambulation of a shrine once the pilgrim has arrived is another

common ritual pattern, as if the pilgrim were trying to encompass the

bounds of the shrine, taking in the edges before approaching the center.

—Jean Dalby Clift and Wallace B. Clift, *The Archetype of*
  Pilgrimage: Outer Action with Inner Meaning

Circumambulation sometimes feels so very right.
Although part of me always wants to go and get directly on the
    labyrinth's path,
at times a wiser part leads me to approach differently.

Once,
walking around the inside of the cathedral
appreciating the windows, the pillars, the arches,
and the rich sense of collected prayers,
increased my appetite
for a very nourishing and delicious meal of labyrinth praying.

Another time,
moving counterclockwise around the labyrinth's perimeter seven times
broke up the soil within me
so that seeds of growth and healing could be planted
as I moved on the labyrinth's terrain.

Circling clockwise seven times around the labyrinth when I came out
seemed to be a way of protecting and watering
what had been planted.

And Jesus told them many things in parables,
saying: "Listen! A sower went out to sow. And as he
sowed, some seeds fell on the path, and the birds
came and ate them up. Other seeds fell on rocky
ground, where they did not have much soil, and they
sprang up quickly, since they had no depth of soil.
But when the sun rose, they were scorched; and since

they had no root, they withered away. Other seeds fell
among thorns, and the thorns grew up and choked
them. Other seeds fell on good soil and brought forth
grain, some a hundredfold, some sixty, some thirty.
Let anyone with ears listen!" (Matthew 13:3–9)

WANDERING WITH PURPOSE

Say or think: "perimeter, edges, center," once or many times. What words,
feelings, music, sensations, or images are presenting themselves?

Medieval pilgrims
slept on the floor
of Chartres Cathedral.

I wonder what dreams I would have
if I spent the night
with my ear pressed against the floor,
against the labyrinth.

> For God speaks in one way, and in two,
> though people do not perceive it. In a dream,
> in a vision of the night, when deep sleep falls on
> mortals, while they slumber on their beds,
> then God opens their ears. (Job 33:14–16a)

SACRED DREAMING

Pray, asking God to communicate with you as you sleep tonight.

After dinner several from our group go to the cathedral
to uncover the labyrinth
in preparation for our walk.
(The whole group will put the chairs back "in place"
when we are done.)

When we were asked, "Who would like to prepare the space
for our group walk of the labyrinth?"
like an eager second grader I waved my hand, "ME! ME! ME!"
I knew that this type of spiritual service would be a gift to me.

What a privilege to take the chairs off the labyrinth!
I volunteered for this "job,"
but I knew it would be pure joy, not just work!

There's nothing very extraordinary about our actions—
we approach a row of five chairs which are connected, then
lift, move, set down; lift, move, set down; lift, move, set down . . .

Yet our clearing away feels like a gift to this beautiful friend.
As each row of chairs is placed out of the way
the space around the labyrinth seems more alive.
A sense of opening radiates from the floor, extending outward.
It is almost as if the labyrinth is breathing more freely.

Do not lag in zeal, be ardent in spirit, serve God.
(Romans 12:11)

Taking Action

If you could offer any gift of spiritual service, what would you do? Get going!

We place the small red plastic holders
filled with white votive candles
around the outside of the labyrinth.

We light the candles
with hope.

We ask for God's presence to be experienced.
We ask for the companionship of God's light.
We ask God for gifts of openness and insight.

We also light the candles
out of our sense of assurance.

We know God is present.
We trust in God's transforming power.
We act on our faith
as we pray with our feet
walking the labyrinth.

It is you who light up my lamp;
God, my God, illumines my night.
(Psalm 18:28)

DIVINE LIGHT

What hopes and assurances support your movements of faith?

Our group met at a side door.
We were ushered into the crypt
where the "keeper of the cathedral keys" gave us a lecture
about the history of Chartres Cathedral and its labyrinth.

Below the cathedral,
below the labyrinth,
in the crypt
is the well of Saint Modeste.

Many comments intrigue me:
This well, a holy site, once sat on the top of the hill.
Now it is one hundred and ten feet deep.
The well was used in ancient times for varied purposes.
During battles, many martyrs were thrown into it.
For centuries it has been covered.

The smell of mineral-laden mud draws me to the side of the well.
I look down, down, down,
wondering
"How does the energy of this well
interface with the energy of the labyrinth upstairs?"

Jesus came to a Samaritan city called Sychar,
near the plot of ground that Jacob had given to his son
Joseph. Jacob's well was there, and Jesus, tired out by
his journey, was sitting by the well. It was about noon.

A Samaritan woman came to draw water,
and Jesus said to her, "Give me a drink."
(His disciples had gone to the city to buy food.)

The Samaritan woman said to him, "How is it that
you, a Jew, ask a drink of me, a woman of Samaria?"
(Jews do not share things in common with Samaritans.)

Jesus answered her, "If you knew the gift of God, and who it is that is saying to you, 'Give me a drink,' you would have asked him, and he would have given you living water."

The woman said to him, "Sir, you have no bucket, and the well is deep. Where do you get that living water? Are you greater than our ancestor Jacob, who gave us the well, and with his sons and his flocks drank from it?"

Jesus said to her, "Everyone who drinks of this water will be thirsty again, but those who drink of the water that I will give them will never be thirsty. The water that I will give will become in them a spring of water gushing up to eternal life." (John 4:5–14)

GAZING DOWNWARD

What is underneath the labyrinth that you are walking? What are you sensing about the connections?

Tonight we are walking the labyrinth
processional-style.

Lining up single file down in the crypt, three feet apart,
passing the catechists' baptismal font,
climbing the steps to the main level,
circumambulating all the way around the inside of the sanctuary,
entering the mouth of the labyrinth,
winding our way to the center,
turning toward the altar,
walking in a straight line across the path to it, and
singing our prayers there,
we are doing something familiar in a new way.

I watch the snaking movement of bodies on the path of the labyrinth.

I relax into this different expression of a beloved spiritual practice.

I feel the power of collective experience.

I hear our voices harmonize and reverberate.

Gratitude wells up in me;
it gushes out as I join the others singing "Amazing Grace"!

> From Jesus' fullness we have all received,
> grace upon grace. (John 1:16)

AMAZING GRACE

Recall a deeply meaningful spiritual experience. Involve as many of your senses as possible as you remember it. Bask in your feelings and thoughts. When the time is right, sing "Amazing Grace" or another song that expresses your gratitude.

Processing through the labyrinth "in step,"
three feet between me
and the pilgrim in front
and the pilgrim in back,
helps me to be present to the movement that I see beneath my feet.

The beauty of our bodies
winding this way,
doubling back,
moving across,
turning in time,
heightens my awareness
of the Divine flow of energy within and around us.

The gentle and strong flow of our walking on the path—
as natural as breathing out
and breathing in—
is wondrous to experience and behold.

Your solemn processions are seen, O God,
the processions of my God, my Sovereign, into the
sanctuary—the singers in front, the musicians last,
between them girls playing tambourines.
(Psalm 68:24–25)

WORSHIPING

How have experiences of shared prayer moved you (literally or figuratively)?

Going back to the labyrinth
I place my bare feet
on the flagstones.

A simple gesture,
skin on rock.

I touch more than the floor;
I touch the holy intentions of
other pilgrims
who came before me.

Devotion,
expectation,
love,
and hope
oozed out of their pores,
just as they do out of mine.

Skin on rock, but more.
Spirit above and spirit below.
They exchange a holy kiss.

Whose feet smoothed
the path I follow?

When will someone else connect
with the faith I now walk?

Now faith is the assurance of things hoped for,
the conviction of things not seen. (Hebrews 11:1)

MOVING TOGETHER

Whose spiritual journeys do you touch as you move with God?

Upon entering the labyrinth
I pay attention
to the varied ways in which
I am moving.

My feet choose a meditative pace.
My breath supports my movement.
My muscles move fluidly as I bend, lean, twist, and stretch.
My eyes focus gently on the path right before me.
My mind is quiet and receptive;
it welcomes the thoughts that come without pondering them.

In God we live and move and have our being.
(Acts 17:28a)

Noticing from the Inside Out

Identify the ways in which your body is supporting your spiritual quest. Express what you are discovering.

Intuitive invitations abound
(slow down;
move your arms;
walk backwards;
get off the path;
repeat a line from a song)
as I walk the winding pathway.

When I think about them
(Why should I do that?
What will people think?)
or analyze what they might mean
(Why would I want to do that?
How will this help me get closer to God?)
I become disoriented.

When I respond to them with trust
I feel the welcome power
of swimming with a strong current.

I slept, but my heart was awake. Listen! my beloved is knocking. "Open to me, my sister, my love, my dove, my perfect one; for my head is wet with dew, my locks with the drops of the night." I had put off my garment; how could I put it on again? I had bathed my feet; how could I soil them? My beloved thrust his hand into the opening, and my inmost being yearned for him. I arose to open to my beloved, and my hands dripped with myrrh, my fingers with liquid myrrh, upon the handles of the bolt. I opened to my beloved, but my beloved had turned and was gone. My soul failed me when he spoke. I sought him, but did not find him; I called him, but he gave no answer.

I adjure you, O daughters of Jerusalem, if you find my beloved, tell him this: I am faint with love. (Song of Songs 5:2–6, 8)

TRUSTING

What helps you to flow with your intuition?

Having walked the labyrinth
and needing some time to reflect
I am sitting on the stairs by the altar.
Sensing a desire to respond to my experience,
I take out my pens and drawing pad.
I breathe deeply, waiting expectantly.

Looking up
my eyes are immediately drawn to four white doves
set in beautiful blue stained glass windows.

I take out a red marker and draw a large circle.
In the center I watch my hand create a purple oval.
Around it a rich blue circle grows as I swirl the pen.
Off to the side I place squiggles of deep green.

I look at the drawing recognizing nothing.
I gaze within seeing fullness without form.
"What did this labyrinth walk mean to me?" I ask myself.
My knowing seems as real as it is elusive.

In time I will be able to explain.
From experience I trust that later
I will understand what God has been communicating to me
through my walking of the labyrinth and my drawing.

I shake my head, amazed at the creative process of perceiving.
I bow my head and utter a simple, "Thank you . . .
even though I am not sure what for!"

But, as it is written, "What no eye has seen, nor ear heard,
nor the human heart conceived, what God has prepared for
those who love God"—these things God has revealed
to us through the Spirit; for the Spirit searches everything,
even the depths of God. (1 Corinthians 2:9–10)

KNOWING THE MYSTERY

Draw the first image that pops into your mind. Put down your writing utensil. What are you perceiving? After several moments, offer the prayer that is stirring within you.

She asks,
"How are you doing
after walking the labyrinth
in Chartres last night?"

A laugh of inexplicable joy
bursts forth from my belly.

Without thinking I blurt out,
"I'm doing great! I should be!
It isn't every day that
one of my dreams comes true!"

I laugh again expressing
incredulity and deep gratitude.

> In your presence there is fullness of joy; in your
> right hand are pleasures forevermore. (Psalm 16:11b)

JOY

Recall and savor an experience of intense spiritual joy. Inhale deeply, letting the memory fill you. Where in your body do you feel its memory?

Sometimes I come
not to walk,
but to sit with
the labyrinth.

I look at it,
wondering why its stones
are in such disrepair.

Smatterings of orange spray paint—
markers for the rows of chairs
—dot its ancient flagstones.

The dark center whose covering was removed in wartime
has pieces of exposed metal which have been worn smooth.

I grieve that such a beautiful expression of God's love
has been dishonored by neglect.

Restoration of the labyrinth—
always a possibility
—is becoming
one of the dreams
my heart longs to hold.

So the king said to me, "Why is your face sad, since you
are not sick? This can only be sadness of the heart." Then I
was very much afraid. I said to the king, "May the king live forever! Why should my face not be sad, when the city, the place
of my ancestors' graves, lies waste, and its gates have been
destroyed by fire?" Then the king said to me, "What do you
request?" So I prayed to the God of heaven. Then I said to the
king, "If it pleases the king, and if your servant has found favor
with you, I ask that you send me to Judah, to the city of my
ancestors' graves, so that I may rebuild it." (Nehemiah 2:2–5)

HONORING DIVINE MESSENGERS

As you feel the reverberations of God's love, what dreams are forming within you?

Writers note
that Chartres Cathedral
has the ability to lift
those who enter her.

I experience this
as I come through the doors.
I stand taller;
my spirit soars.

The labyrinth invites me
to stay grounded.
It insists I remain connected
with the Ground of My Being.

The architecture
pulls me up
while the winding path
holds me down.

I feel
the integrity—
the integration—
of the two forces working together.

Blessed are those who trust in God, whose trust
is God. They shall be like a tree planted by water,
sending out its roots by the stream. It shall not fear
when heat comes, and its leaves shall stay green;
in the year of drought it is not anxious, and it
does not cease to bear fruit. (Jeremiah 17:7–8)

INTEGRITY AND INTEGRATION

What does integrity feel like to you? What does integration feel like to you? How do they work together in your body and life?

Tears gently stroke my cheeks
as I consider
Bernard de Clairveaux's poem.
He wrote about his relationship with Jesus' mother;
his words speak to me of something very different.

"When you follow her
you cannot take a wrong turning;
When you pray to her,
you cannot lose hope;
When she fills your thoughts
you are sheltered from all error;
When she holds you up,
you cannot fall;
When she protects you,
you are never afraid;
When she leads you forward,
you are never tired;
When her grace shines on you,
you arrive at your goal."

I cry
because at last I have heard words
which express my experience of walking the labyrinth
and apprehending the beauty of God.

You show me the path of life. (Psalm 16:11a)

SOURCES

What has the power to move you to tears? Write a poem, create a drawing, or find another way to express what you are feeling.

I'm told
that because the path is already set,
"Will I go in, or not?"
is the only choice
that needs to be made
while walking a labyrinth.

But there are many choices of which
I am aware as I walk.

Do I want to use this prayer-walk to consider a pressing concern
or simply to be open to whatever comes?
Will I act on intuitive urges to express myself with body movements?
Will I embrace, resist, or simply notice insights that flash into my head?
What pace suits what I'm experiencing right now?
Do I want to step off the path to let someone by?
Would it be most useful to look up, down, or out?
How long do I want to linger in the center?

I love the choices I make as I walk.
They remind me that as I travel with God
things develop
and change.

God seems to delight in my responsiveness,
matching mental and physical shifts with new invitations.
I find it so enjoyable to share time and space
with a God who is so involved.

Who are they that fear God? God will teach them
the way that they should choose. (Psalm 25:12)

CHOOSING FREELY

Identify recent mental or physical shifts. In what ways did you become aware of God's involvement in your mind, body, and experience?

"Be ready to receive what comes,"
I hear the author of a book about labyrinths say.

What great advice for labyrinth walkers!

So much can come during a labyrinth walk—
self-awareness,
insight,
answers to prayers,
resistance,
memories,
ideas,
a sense of God's presence,
tears,
longings,
sensations of pain,
hopes,
powerful awareness,
new dreams,
images,
songs,
concern for others,
release,
visions,
commitment—
the list is as varied as the walkers.

It is not always easy to be ready to perceive what comes.
That's why I pray for openness and courage.

Wait for God; be strong, and let your heart
take courage; wait for God! (Psalm 27:14)

ASKING FOR HELP

Record the feelings and thoughts that you experience when you consider praying, "God, help me to be open to You." If it feels right, ask for openness.

"...construction of sacred space...
...ratios that help us vibrate...
...proper resonation..."

The lecture on labyrinths is fascinating.
I'm hearing mathematical language
used to describe physical spaces
filled with spiritual opportunity.

Labyrinths are understandable
in so many different ways.

They are
symbols,
spiritual tools,
mathematical images,
harmonic patterns,
pathways of discovery,
playgrounds of prayer.

I want to go
look at the labyrinth
on the floor of Chartres Cathedral again.

What will I perceive
if I see with eyes
informed by new perspectives?

Some people brought a blind man to Jesus and begged him to touch him. Jesus took the blind man by the hand and led him out of the village; and when he had put saliva on his eyes and laid his hands upon him, he asked him, "Can you see anything?" And the man looked up and said, "I can see people, but they look like trees, walking." Then Jesus laid his hands on his eyes again; and he looked intently and his sight was restored, and he saw everything clearly. (Mark 8:22–25)

SAME SCENE, DIFFERENT ANGLES

What do you need to look at again? What will you perceive if you see with eyes informed by new perspectives?

I am stunned.

The rector of Chartres Cathedral
is explaining the medieval context
of the labyrinth in Chartres.

Back in the 1200s people believed
that children formed in their mothers' intestines.
Father Legaux is asking us to wonder about the
intestine-like design of the Chartres labyrinth.

My breath is taken away
as he notes that the number of stones
on the winding way of the labyrinth
matches exactly the number of days
that medieval folks believed
it took for a baby to form.

I can't explain why this feels so profound to me.
Yet I am overwhelmed with the sense that
I am listening to something that is truly significant.

Blessed be the God . . . of our Savior Jesus Christ!
By God's great mercy God has given us a new birth
into a living hope through the resurrection of Jesus
Christ from the dead, and into an inheritance that is
imperishable, undefiled, and unfading, kept in heaven
for you, who are being protected by the power of God
through faith for a salvation ready to be revealed in the
last time. In this you rejoice. (1 Peter 1:3–6a)

GESTATION

Visualize a smooth pathway of creativity flowing through your life. How would your experience of it change if you see that it is composed of hundreds of individual stones?

"All who walk the labyrinth
are on the same path with the same goal,"
the rector preaches.

He continues,
"There is always a time when you go by someone
moving in the opposite direction.
Don't be fooled by appearance.
Whether heading in to the center
or heading out from the center
you are both on the same path."

I'm eating up his every word!
What I'm hearing is that
the labyrinth is a tool of compassion
through which we can learn to accept things that seem opposite
but are not.
It is a place where the bigger picture of life
can come into clearer focus.

Having heard these words,
I am more eager than ever
to walk the labyrinth again.

> As God's chosen ones, holy and beloved, clothe
> yourselves with compassion, kindness, humility,
> meekness, and patience. Bear with one another and,
> if anyone has a complaint against another, forgive
> each other; just as God has forgiven you, so you also
> must forgive. Above all, clothe yourselves with love,
> which binds everything together in perfect harmony.
> (Colossians 3:12–14)

The Way of Compassion

What opposites have you noticed or experienced lately? As you pray, remembering them and feeling ready to understand them in new ways, how are you changing?

During our last day in the town of Chartres
a labyrinth maker,
this time adding a new dimension to our discussion of sacred geometry,
lectures on-site about the construction of the cathedral.
I listen as I gaze at the labyrinth.

We are told that the cathedral
and the labyrinth
are "visual examples of what we hear in harmony."

"The labyrinth is singing a divine love song to us,"
flashes through my mind.
I recognize it by sight.
I have felt its rhythms.
Now I pray for ears to hear it as well.

Let anyone with ears to hear listen! (Mark 4:9)

DIVINE HARMONY

What love song is God singing to you?

We will be leaving the town of Chartres in thirty minutes.
I am waiting at the cathedral when the doors are unlocked.

Walking directly to the labyrinth
I place the multicolored blanket I use during prayer
in the center
and sit down.

I feel
harmony,
an unidentifiable vibration,
and Love.

Full of longing
to pray with this beautiful labyrinth many more times,
I gather my gratitude,
which seems to want to radiate from my hands, my mind, my feet, and
my heart.

It is time to go . . .
I stand and bow.
I pray the only thing that makes sense:
"Thank you, God of the labyrinth."

> O give thanks to God, call on God's name, make
> known God's deeds among the peoples. Sing to God,
> sing praises to God; tell of all God's wonderful works.
> (Psalm 105:1–2)

GIVING THANKS

Express your gratitude to God in a way that feels natural to you.

CHARTRES

Bolen, Jean Shinoda. "Quickening: Chartres Cathedral." In *Crossing to Avalon: A Woman's Mid-life Pilgrimage*. San Francisco: HarperSanFrancisco, 1994.

Charpentier, Louis. *The Mysteries of Chartres Cathedral*. Translated by Ronald Fraser in collaboration with Janette Jackson. London: Thorsons Publishers Ltd., 1966.

Houvet, Etienne. *Chartres Cathedral*. Chartres, France: Editions Houvet-la Crypte, 1996.

Macaulay, David. *Cathedral*. Boston: Houghton Mifflin, 1973.

Péguy, Charles. *Chartres*. St. Léger Vauban, France: Zodiac, 1983.

"The Powers behind Chartres" and "The Symbolism of Chartres." In *The Atlas of Mysterious Places: The World's Unexplained Sacred Sites, Symbolic Landscapes, Ancient Cities and Lost Lands*, edited by Jennifer Westwood. New York: Weidenfeld & Nicolson, 1987.

CREATIVITY

Cameron, Julia. *The Vein of Gold: A Journey to Your Creative Heart*. New York: G. P. Putnam's Sons, 1996.

Cameron, Julia, and Mark Bryan. *The Artist's Way: A Spiritual Path to Higher Creativity*. New York: G. P. Putnam's Sons, 1992.

Collins, Tracy. "A Discussion of Voice." *The Brown Papers* 3, no. 8 (May 1997): 1–15.

Fincher, Susanne F. *Creating Mandalas for Insight, Healing, and Self-Expression*. Boston: Shambhala, 1991.

Velasco, Angelito. *El Diario Personal: Un Cominzo* (A Journal: A Beginning). Translated by Franklin Curbelo. St. Paul, Minn.: Compas, 1996.

Walker, Alice, Isabel Allende, and Jean Shinoda Bolen. "Giving Birth, Finding Form." Boulder, Colo.: Sounds True Recordings, 1993.

LABYRINTHS

Artress, Lauren. *Walking a Sacred Path: Rediscovering the Labyrinth as a Spiritual Tool.* New York: Riverhead Books, 1995.

Aviva, Elyn. "Seeking the Center: Pilgrimages and Labyrinths as Sacred Journeys." Unpublished paper, American Academy of Religion, San Francisco, 1997.

Bourgeois, Jean-Louis. "Surprise! The Seven-Circuit Labyrinth, Chartres, and the Harmonists." *Labyrinth Letter* 3, no. 4 (October 1997): 4–8.

Cain, Marty. "Tools for Life: A Search." *Labyrinth Letter* 1, no. 1 (April 1995): 12–14.

Campbell, Scott. "Mazes and Labyrinths. A Search for the Center." Scottsdale, Ariz.: Lutz Limited, 1996.

Coffey, Kathy. "Labyrinth Prayer." *Praying* 64 (January–February 1995): 20.

Ellard, Peter. "The Theology of the School of Chartres and the Labyrinth of Chartres Cathedral." Unpublished paper. American Academy of Religion, San Francisco, November 1997.

Fairchild, Kristen. "Veriditas and the Worldwide Labyrinth Project." http://www.gracecathedral.org/veriditas/features/vision.shtml (1997): 1–16.

Kidd, Sue Monk. "A Guiding Feminine Myth." In *The Dance of the Dissident Daughter.* San Francisco: HarperSanFrancisco, 1996.

Koch, Cathy. "Labyrinth Laborer: St. Charles' Episcopal Church." *Labyrinth Letter* 2, no. 1 (January 1996): 20–21.

"Labyrinth: The History of the Maze." Washington, D.C.: New River Media, 1996.

Laishley, Barbara. "The Labyrinth as Ritual Action: An Examination of Efficacy, Intent, and Neurological Function." Unpublished paper. American Academy of Religion, San Francisco, November 1997.

Lanser, Taffy. "Grace Cathedral Labyrinth: A Rug beneath My Feet." *Labyrinth Letter* 1, no. 1 (April 1995): 11.

Lindsay, Tamar. "What's in a Name? Choices in the Unicursal Labyrinth. The Path versus the Wall." Parts 1 and 2. *Labyrinth Letter* 2, no. 2 (January 1996): 2–4; no. 3 (July 1996): 4–7.

Lonegren, Sig. "The Benton Castle Labyrinth." *Labyrinth Letter* 2, no. 4 (October 1996): 10–13.

———. "The Classical Seven Circuit Labyrinth: Coming to Terms." *Labyrinth Letter* 1, no. 1 (April 1995): 4–7.

———. *Labyrinths: Ancient Myths and Modern Uses.* Glastonbury, U.K.: Gothic Image Publications, 1996.

"Mazes and Labyrinths: The Search for the Center." Video. Cyclone Productions, 1996.

"Mazes and Labyrinths: Symbols of the Soul." In *The Atlas of Mysterious Places: The World's Unexplained Sacred Sites, Symbolic Landscapes, Ancient Cities, and Lost Lands*, edited by Jennifer Westwood. New York: Weidenfeld & Nicolson, 1987.

McMillen, Joan. "Remembering the Way: Ceremony in Honor of the Labyrinth at Chartres." Menlo Park, Calif.: Joan Marie McMillen, 1989.

Oppenheimer, Max, Jr. "On Labyrinths and Mazes—Meanderings and Musings." *Labyrinth Letter* 1, no. 2 (July 1995): 4–6.

Saward, Jeff. "Ancient Labyrinths of the World." Parts 1–6. *Labyrinth Letter* 2, no. 2 (April 1996): 6–9; no. 3 (July 1996): 8–11; no. 4 (October 1996): 4–7; *Labyrinth Letter* 3, no. 1 (January 1997): 4–6; no. 3 (July 1997): 4–7; no. 4 (October 1997): 10–15.

Shields, Carol. *Larry's Party*. New York: Viking, 1997.

Weber, Susan. "What Is a Labyrinth?" *Labyrinth Letter* 2, no. 1 (January 1996): 24.

PILGRIMAGE

Bolen, Jean Shinoda. *Crossing to Avalon: A Woman's Mid-Life Pilgrimage*. San Francisco: HarperSanFrancisco, 1994.

Clift, Jean Dalby, and Wallace B. Clift. *The Archetype of Pilgrimage: Outer Action with Inner Meaning*. Mahwah, N.J.: Paulist Press, 1996.

Colinon, Maurice. *Guide des Monastères*. Paris: Pierre Horay Editeur, 1995.

Cousineau, Phil. "The Art of Pilgrimage: Soulful Travel in an Age of Hyperspeed." *Connections* 1, no. 1 (September 1997): 20–21.

Dougherty, Rose Mary. "Looking for Speed Traps." *Shalem News* 21, no. 2 (summer 1997): 9.

Lane, Beldane. *Landscapes of the Sacred: Geography and Narrative in American Spirituality*. New York: Paulist Press, 1988.

Marty, Martin, and Micah Marty. *Places along the Way: Meditations on the Journey of Faith*. Minneapolis: Augsburg, 1994.

May, Gerald. "Don't Be a Pest: Counsels for Spiritual Directors from John of the Cross." *Shalem News* 21, no. 2 (summer 1997): 5.

Rausch, Sheila. "The Sacrament of Now." *Benedictine Sisters and Friends* 1, no. 3 (summer 1997): 4–5.

Robinson, Martin. *Sacred Places, Pilgrim Paths*. London: HarperCollins, 1997.